Introduction

Welcome to your new life as a witty person. Even if the words that best describe you right now might be 'shy', 'introverted', or even the dreaded 'boring' understand this: you *can* become the kind of person that people want to be around (unless of course you smell, but I can't help you with that). While it may be true that it is very difficult to change ones innate personality, your transformation into a witty person is something that can be done methodically and easily over a matter of a few months, or even weeks. It is a gradual transformation, it doesn't involve a full moon or a secret potion, and as an added bonus it doesn't even hurt.

I realize that if you consider yourself a shy person, changing your personality in such a radical way may sound like a huge undertaking. Being a shy person is an obstacle that may even seem insurmountable to you. But stop for a moment and consider *why* you are a shy person. Most people are shy because they don't feel that they have anything worthwhile to say in a conversation. If you believe that nothing you say will be of any value to anyone, you are probably not going to say much of anything. The difference is that after you learn this system, you *will* have worthwhile things to say — things that will make other people laugh. When you start making people laugh, you will realize what a good feeling it is to have that power. And you *will* say more. Before you know it, one day you will look up and realize that you are no longer a shy person. There won't be a conscious change, it will just happen while you are applying the techniques of this system.

Besides, if you are reading this then you *want* to change. Wanting it is the most important motivation you need if you are going to change your personality. Remember, what the human mind can conceive and believe it can achieve. Now, look what you've done, you've made me go all Tony Robbins. This is not a hard process to follow. I'm not asking you to crawl on your knees for five miles uphill through broken glass…it's more like riding a bicycle for five miles on level ground. That's probably hard enough for most of us out-of-shape people to do!

This is a simple, methodical system to follow. If you learn the techniques described in this book you *will* become witty when you put them into practice. It can't be helped! If you can have a conversation with someone, you can be witty. And you have conversations with people every day! Take each chapter and absorb the material. Periodically, some chapters will give you exercises to do (which I call 'Lab Work'). These exercises will pave the way as you start down the road to your new life. As you will learn in this book, the ability to be witty is not some intangible quality that eludes explanation like musical talent or writing ability. It is a tangible, learnable skill that can be gained through the use of a few simple techniques. You can start off with just a little skill, or none at all. The result is the same. Above all, enjoy the process!

Chapter 1
The Evolution of the Science of Wit

The well of true wit is truth itself. -George Meredith

I'll start off by giving you a little history on how I came to develop this system.

The science of wit all started almost 20 years ago when I was working as a delivery driver at KFC. I worked with a cook named Mike. Now, Mike was the kind of guy that had a funny line or witty remark for every subject you could think of. And I do mean every subject. I truly don't remember a single conversation we had without getting some kind of funny remark after every sentence. This guy was incredible.

The really amazing thing was the speed at which he would do this. There was no pause at all between the time you stopped talking and the time he would come out with his line. I would often just listen to him talk to other people and marvel at his ability to do this. Like most people, I always thought that his skill was something he was born with, that there was no way I could learn to be that sharp. I learned later that I was wrong.

I was always a bit of an introvert. I always found it hard to meet new people or engage in small talk or simple conversation. Needless to say, I was certainly not someone you would call witty. So when I saw how effortlessly Mike could do all the things I could not, I was envious, to say the least. I often thought that if I could just have one tenth of the ability that Mike had, it would make my life a hundred times better.

One day, long after I had left that job, I was sitting around thinking about younger days when I recalled Mike and his talents. As I wondered how he did what he did it suddenly occurred to me that if I could in fact succeed in deconstructing how someone might be witty, it would follow that the skill could be learned. Armed with this belief, I set out to discover the step-by-step process to learn to be witty.

Following my admittedly limited knowledge of the scientific method, I began with a basic assumption that there had to be a specific set of steps that I could employ to actually change my personality from shy to witty. I started by defining the qualities that someone would need to have to make them a witty person, then broke those qualities down into their component pieces. I then studied how one could gain each quality, and after some time I had a step to achieve each one.

And an amazing thing happened. The more I studied and analyzed the process, the more I came to understand that the method really could be learned, that this was *not* an innate quality that you had to be born with. Using the qualities I reasoned one would need, I created a formula that had the necessary ingredients to produce wit. Once I had the formula of wit, it was just a matter of putting the formula into practice, and the science of wit was born. Of course, being a mad scientist, I had to try the formula on myself first.

It worked! As the weeks passed, I could feel myself literally *becoming* that witty person. The change was gradual, but very powerful. Suddenly, I was making people laugh in the conversations I was having with them, be it at work, at the coffee shop, buying clothes, *everywhere*. What a powerful feeling! With every passing day I could feel myself becoming more and more confident and at ease with the simple act of making conversation. Meeting people was easier, and people were starting to enjoy talking to me. I loved making people laugh, and people loved laughing with me. And, it should be emphasized, *I have extreme stage fright*.

What did he just say? You heard right, I am deathly afraid of public speaking, even to this day. I have been known to quit school courses because I had to make presentations to the class, and I have only made two speeches in my entire life—one at my best friend's wedding (I had to, I was the best man), and one at my own wedding (there's no way to get out of that one). I did well when I did make the speeches, but I absolutely hated it with a passion. If you're like most people, you probably feel the same way. One statistic says that more people are afraid of public speaking than of death (of course, 80% of all statistics are made up on the spot). But the point is that you can become a witty person without having to be an entertainer.

Eventually, I made it close to the level that Mike was at. However, only once I was there did I realize that having a line for absolutely everything becomes just a little bit too much of a good thing. Realizing this, I scaled it back, and these days I maintain it at a comfortable level that keeps people laughing just enough. There can be such a thing as too much wit. You don't want to cross the line between being funny and just being a smartass.

So don't worry if you think you can't do it -realize that if I can do it, you can as well. You don't have to be a performer or a comedian. This is not a show, you don't have to be an actor--you are simply conversing in a normal manner. The only difference is that what you will be saying once you are witty will be very different than what you say now. Like anything worthwhile, it takes work, but the rewards are well worth it. Just remember, never take yourself too seriously--have fun at it!

Chapter 2
What is Wit?

Wit is the sudden marriage of ideas which before their union were not perceived to have any relation. -Mark Twain

Chances are, you've met people who are witty. These are the people who always seem to have something funny to say, no matter what the situation is that they are in. People that seem to have an endless supply of funny comments which they can produce effortlessly at any given moment. People that other people want to talk to; people who always have a crowd around them at parties. If this already describes you, then why are you reading this? Get to a party! If this doesn't describe you, then hopefully this book will show you how you can become that witty person.

But who are these people? Are they professional comedians? Are they superintelligent beings who practice an art that we mere mortals could never hope to achieve? Have they studied for years under Tibetan monks, learning the ancient ways of the sacred punchline? No, these are people just like you and me, doctors, factory workers, taxi drivers, waiters, and yes, even accountants. To most of these people the talent of wit comes naturally. They don't have to think about how they do what they do, it is something that is innate in their personality. In time it will be just as automatic for you, too. The techniques in this book are not difficult to use, but they do require a commitment of at least some of your time, at least while you are learning the system. Like anything else, the change can come either quickly or slowly, it all depends on how much effort you want to put into it.

Is being witty an art? No. Notice that this book is not called 'The Art of Wit'. The ability to make art is something that you are born with, an intangible quality that allows one person to see things in a different way from other people and express themselves in painting, music, or some other creative endeavor. Anyone can learn the basic skills of the mechanics of making art, but if they lack that inner intangible quality of the artist, their works will probably not be considered as art by any discerning collector. In other words, even a monkey can be taught to paint, but he's not going to create the Mona Lisa anytime soon. Well, unless there's an infinite number of monkeys…but then they would be too busy writing Shakespeare to paint. The point is, you can be taught how to draw, but it takes innate skill to become an artist.

This book is called "The Science of Wit" because the ability to be witty *is* a science. It is not something that you have to be born with, it is a simple formula that can easily be learned and put into practice by anyone, the same way that anyone can learn how to cook. Sure, some people will be better than others, and right now you might be such a bad cook that your family prays *after* they eat, but anyone can learn to mix ingredients, and that's just about how hard it is to learn this formula. So don't worry, if you follow the instructions in this book you will learn to be that witty, funny person you want to be.

But what is wit? The dictionary describes wit as "the ability to relate seemingly disparate things so as to illuminate or amuse". What does this mean exactly? You're asking the wrong person, there's a lot of really big words there. What I think it means is that no matter what subject comes up in a conversation, a witty person can come out with a funny line either about that subject, or take something else that might be funny and relate it to that subject. For example, when you are having a conversation with someone and they happen to say that they are going bowling tomorrow, you can come out with a line like "Oh, I gave up bowling for sex...the balls are lighter and you don't have to change your shoes." This, being an unexpected thing for someone to say, causes the people listening to laugh. But how was this accomplished? You guessed it, you related two seemingly disparate things (in this case bowling and sex) in such a way as to illuminate or amuse the listener. This is the essence of wit.

But let's talk for a minute about expectation. In the science of wit, expectation is the equivalent of absolute zero—the temperature when particles of humor stop colliding with quantum waves of unpredictability to produce laughter. Or something like that. Either way, expectation is something to be avoided at all costs. To understand this, it is necessary to discuss why someone laughs in the first place.

There are many theories written by actual scientists on why human beings laugh. Probably no one knows for sure, but what follows is my personal theory (backed by extremely complicated research involving a few mice and a tiny stand-up microphone).

When someone laughs, it is usually because something unexpected has either happened or has been said. This is for two reasons. First, when something completely unexpected occurs in front of us, a rush of adrenaline courses through your body and your muscles become tense. This is a primal reaction that prepares your body for the so-called "flight or fight" response. This is a response that developed as cavemen, and it is there so that when you come around the side of a rock and Thontag is waiting there with a club to thump your head and take your mammoth hide from you, your body is ready to either run or fight even before you brain can recognize whether or not the situation is hostile.

Because your body is ready to go before your brain can actually process the event, what do you think happens when your eyes and brain tell you 'hey, Thontag's not carrying a club, he's playing air guitar to ABBA with the leg bone from an allosaurus'? Well, what happens is that the brain has to put the energy somewhere, and there's no reason to run or to fight, so the brain does the only thing left—the excess energy that your body has goes into laughter because the scene is so unexpected. Now, this is entirely my theory and is probably so full of holes you could use it for a screen door, but the end result is the same...when confronted with something so entirely unexpected as a caveman playing a bone, you just have to laugh. The second reason a person laughs at unexpected events or when someone says something unexpected is because of the image it creates in your mind. So, for example, here we are talking about the science of wit and suddenly, for no reason at all, I say 'Do you think that when the people who work at Dairy Queen take a crap they do that little swirl at the end?' If you laughed, and I hope you did, it's because of the image that was suddenly thrust into your mind out of the blue. It is this lack of expectation and imagery that makes wit work.

We will look a little more into expectation in Chapter 7. For now, just realize that we can make this lack of expectation work for us by injecting funny lines, observations or even movie quotes into a conversation when the listeners least expect it. This is one of the skills that can make you appear witty to other people.

Chapter 3
Why be Witty?

The first ingredient in conversation is truth, the next good sense, the third good humor, and the fourth wit. -William Temple

So, now that we know what it means to be witty, why should we strive to be that way? The answer to that question can only be provided by you. It may be because you are tired of being the quiet, reserved type. It may be that you want to sharpen skills that you may have already started to develop. Whatever the reason, it is quite possible to achieve this goal, and the advantages are many. Once you are witty, you may find yourself invited to more parties, you may find it easier to meet people and develop working or personal relationships that are lasting and rewarding.

The best part about all of this is that the change does not take place overnight. It is a gradual transformation that occurs as you learn the skills and then apply what you have learned. The change itself is an ongoing thing, but you should be well on your way to your new personality in as little as a few weeks. Sorry, there's no magic bean that will grow this personality overnight. I know that's probably not what you want to hear in this age of instant gratification, but the fact that it takes some time is actually a good thing. If the change took place overnight, people would notice and think that you are just putting on an act, and this is absolutely **not** the effect that we want. This is very important because you do not want them to think that your personality is fake--nobody likes a person who appears to be about as genuine as Pamela Anderson's breasts. By making the change evenly and by degrees people will not be able to pinpoint it, they will gradually forget the way you were and just realize that it is fun to have you around, and the best part is, they will almost unconsciously try harder to make sure that you are around.

To start with, you have to decide that this is what you really want. The ability to come out with a snappy remark can have tremendous benefits in your social life, but, as with anything, it takes some dedication in the beginning. After a while it becomes automatic, but at first it may seem a little like work. The payoff is well worth it, though. There can also be a down side as well, albeit a very small one that may never even happen to you. When you develop your skills to the point where it is automatic, you may find that people will sometimes *rely* on your skill. Sometimes, people will invite you to a social event where they expect an awkward situation to develop, such as a blind date or family gathering...because they know tensions might be high and they think that your witty comments will keep a light-hearted atmosphere, thereby diffusing the situation. Sometimes, they will add even more pressure by actually telling you that they expect you to do this. This becomes a high-pressure situation for you, because you have to be "on" for the whole night. Many people shut down in this situation. This will be the hardest situation that you can face, and can be one of the few times that being witty can stop being fun and become real work! It would be a good practice to try and avoid getting yourself into a situation like this if at all possible. If not, try and make the best of it...after all, it is a compliment--you won't get caught in this situation unless you are good at being witty.

For the most part, however, when you hit that perfect line that makes everyone explode into laughter the feeling that comes over you just can't be beat. It's a great feeling to think that people might have just a little more joy simply because they had a conversation with you. In the next chapter we will learn the top secret formula that you can use to make this happen.

Chapter 4
The Formula of Wit

Brevity is the soul of wit. -William Shakespeare

Now that we know the what and the why, we can start on the *how*. As discussed in Chapter 2, the ability to be witty is not something that you have to be born with. It follows a simple formula that is very easy to learn and put into practice. Now, for the first time anywhere in the world, I will reveal the secret formula. Prepare to have your mind, like, expanded, man.

Material + Opportunity + Recall + Delivery = Wit

Booyah! In your face, Einstein. Not as many ingredients as the Colonel's secret recipe, and it won't put caramel in the Caramilk bar, but it does get the job done nicely. Pretty simple, huh? It is just a matter of searching out material, altering the material if necessary, getting or making the opportunity to use the material, recalling the material, and delivering the material for a given situation. You, in the back row...pay attention, there will be a test at the end of this chapter. It may sound difficult, but this is not grade 11 math, people. Remember, even if 4 out of 3 people have problems with fractions, this is not a hard formula to put into practice once it is broken down into bite-sized chunks.

In the coming chapters we will deal with each step of the formula in detail, but here's a synopsis of what's in store for you as you begin your journey.

The first part of the formula deals with material. At this point you may be wondering how you can possibly come up with material if the best thing you have ever written was a grocery list. After all, if you're not witty now, how can you expect to think up material to be witty with? Don't worry. In Chapters 6 and 7 you will learn how to get material from various sources that are all around you. In chapter 8 you will learn how to refine this material. For now, it is enough to know that you don't have to write the material at all…it is everywhere, just waiting for you to harvest and use it. The best part is that when you become proficient at the system, you don't even have to study the material--it comes to you while you are being entertained yourself.

The second part of the formula is opportunity. After all, once you know all this great material you need a place to use it, don't you? Opportunities are around you every day, in nearly every conversation in your day-to-day life, if you are well prepared with material. Remember, luck is when preparation meets opportunity. In the beginning, you are going to have a few great lines, just waiting to come out. You know that these lines will produce good laughs, but haven't had the opportunity to use them yet. At first, you will be passively waiting for the opportunity to present itself, quietly listening to the conversation until a subject comes up that fits your line. This is effective, and it works, but you may find that you have long waits in between opportunities. But as your skills develop and your confidence grows, you will find more and more that you can begin to sense the direction a conversation is going and have a line ready and waiting when it gets to just the right point. At your peak, you will even be able to gently steer conversations towards subjects that you have material for, and nobody will even notice that you are directing the whole process. Chapter 9 goes into more detail on this topic.

The next part of the formula is recall. Once you have the opportunity to use the material, you will need to recall the line that fits the situation you are in. This is not as hard as it sounds, because in order to recognize (or create) the opportunity to use a witty line, you will usually have a line in mind before this point is reached. As you use the techniques presented in this book, you will find that the lines come to mind quicker and quicker, until you can sustain the appearance of having a line for any situation, effortlessly recalled on a moment's notice, which of course makes you look like a star. And isn't that what this is all about? Chapter 10 deals with recall. The last part of the formula is delivery. Perhaps the most important part, but also the easiest to learn. In chapter 11 we will go over the different types of delivery and when to use them.

Using this formula will be a slow process at first, but as you learn and practice, your talents and memory will develop, and you will find that it gets easier and easier. As with anything worthwhile in life, it takes hard work and practice, but in the end the rewards are worth every effort.

Chapter 5
Types of Humor

Don't put too fine a point to your wit for fear it should get blunted. -Miguel de Cervantes Saavedra

There are many different types of humor, but we will only discuss the ones that apply to our mission of making you witty.

The most common type of humor that you will come across is workplace banter. I mention this one first because this is something that you likely hear on a daily basis (you *are* gainfully employed, aren't you?). Banter is the joking and teasing that constantly goes on at work between coworkers. This is a great place to showcase your wit because a wide variety of situations often arises that you can poke fun at. Try not to poke fun at the boss though, or you might be trying to think up witty comments for the unemployment line!

Banter at work usually involves one of two things: poking fun at a particular person or being critical of the organization itself. When you make fun of the organization, everyone is usually on your side, so it can be a great way to endear yourself to the group. For example, when you get your paycheck and open the envelope in front of coworkers you say "great, now I can buy that gumball I always wanted." That's a whole lot funnier than saying "boy, is my paycheck ever small!" Everyone can relate to having a small paycheck. Or try looking disappointed when you open it and saying "I still didn't get that pink slip." These are the small things that contribute to the overall picture of you as a witty person. An important thing to remember is that humor often comes from the *way* you say things, not the actual things you say (if that makes any sense). For example, I could say "my career is going nowhere." Although horribly and painfully true in my case, it's not really funny at all. Instead, it would be better to say, "excuse me, I have to go to the toilet--you know, to visit my career." The same thing was said in a different, unexpected way, which makes it funny.

The other workplace banter involves making fun of someone else. A word of caution here-tread carefully when taking part in this type of workplace banter. You don't want to make fun of someone in the group if you don't know them very well. It will just make you look like a jerk and will not help endear you to the group. Also, try not to make fun of the person who appears to be the most popular member of the group. If, however, they make fun of you first-feel free to hammer them (in a tasteful way, of course). This type of humor must always take a lighthearted tone, never come too close to the truth and never, ever stray into an area where it might be considered harassment, sexual or otherwise.

Another type of humor is self-deprecating humor. This is often one of the best ways to fit in with a group, because if you're attacking yourself, people will more readily laugh than if you attack someone else who may be their friend. Make this your motto: it doesn't matter if they are laughing with you or laughing at you as long as they're laughing. This is an important point. If people are laughing at you-as long as it's not in a malicious way—they are still laughing, and this is the goal. Make them laugh! Another important point is that by making fun of yourself, you send a clear message to the group that this is a person who doesn't take themselves too seriously, someone who is lighthearted, self-assured and above all fun to talk to.

One type of humor that can be funny, but also damaging is sarcasm--be careful with this one. There is a reason why sarcasm is called 'the wit of fools'. Used too much, sarcasm is no longer funny. Instead, it changes people's perception of you from funny to bitter. Used sparingly here and there however, sarcasm can be funny and illuminating.

Situational humor is another type which can be very funny. This type is often the one that raises people's overall perception of you as being witty. This is because the lines that you are saying directly fit the situation you are in. You appear to have perfect timing and an endless supply of material pulled out of your head at a moment's notice. This is one of the best ways to appear witty.

Chapter 6
Sources of Material

Next to being witty, the best thing is being able to quote another's wit. - Christian Nestell Bovee

By now, hopefully, you are saying to yourself, "yes, I want to do this, but where can I get the material I need to appear witty?". I'm glad you asked.

To start with, realize this—you are reading this book because *you are not witty*. Sorry, but that's the harsh reality of it, and if you can accept this fact you are a lot further on your way than you know. Right now, you have no material. You are probably not a writer of comedy, either, so it's not going to be easy to come up with material on your own. Not impossible, but not very easy. Given these facts, we can come up with only one conclusion--you are going to have to use other people's material.

Understand that this is not a bad thing. This is not stealing. You are merely using some funny lines from different sources to appear witty in your personal life. You are not going to be a standup comedian and steal other comedian's acts. This is an important point to remember. **Never** use material from any source other than yourself for financial gain.

One of the best sources of material is stand-up comedy. Find the comedy clubs in your city and go to see the show as often as you can. Comedy clubs usually change comedians every 1-2 weeks, so if you can see each new comedian, you will be very far ahead of the game. While it can be difficult to write anything down in a dark comedy club, even just seeing the show is by far the best way to absorb material.

With any comedian's act, you are going to hear some lines that make you laugh more than others. Make a point of taking a moment after one of these lines to repeat it a few times to yourself. Even if you miss some jokes while you are doing this, you are far more likely to remember a few of these lines after the show. You will find that you start to remember more and more with practice. And don't worry if you don't get any material at all from a show, it happens. Sometimes you only get one good line in a month, but it is still worth checking out the shows. You will find that you start to absorb and emulate the way that comedians act, including their timing and perhaps some of their mannerisms.

Now, a couple of words of warning here. It bears repeating to be aware of the source of your material...if you were to get a live act going or write an article or book, you would be guilty of stealing material from these comedians. It is okay to use comedian's material with your friends, but remember not to steal for commercial gain.

Another warning is this: do not use material from very well-known comedians. The reason for this is that the likelihood is very high that someone you are talking to has heard the line before, and will know that you are using other people's material. THIS MUST BE AVOIDED AT ALL COSTS! Sorry, didn't mean to shout there, but in order to appear witty, you have to appear that *you* have a line for everything, and it must look as if you are making them up on the spot. If you use well-known material you will just look like a parrot. Of course, there are some exceptions to this rule. Sometimes, such as in the case of movie or TV quotes, you may want people to know the reference you are making.

Another source of material is something you probably do a lot of now--watch television. Getting material from television sitcoms allows you to relax in your own home and write down lines that you find especially humorous. A side benefit of sitcoms is the sit part-and I'm not talking about sitting down, I'm talking about situation. A sitcom works by setting up a situation, then having the characters react in a funny way to that situation. If you learn a few lines for different situations, you can begin to recognize these situations when they arise, and deliver the perfect line. Don't forget, there are also a number of shows and even whole networks that showcase standup comedians on a regular basis. This can save you a trip to the comedy club and expose you to a larger variety of comedians.

As always, there are things to watch out for when using sitcom material, or any other material from television. First of all, the same rules apply as getting material from comedians--do not use this material for commercial gain. The other hazard to watch out for is to *not use the line right away*. This is not always easy. It is very tempting to come out with a line you heard the night before on a popular sitcom or comedy show, but the chance is just too great that someone will have heard the same line last night, and again they will know that you are not being original. Remember, in order for you to appear witty, it has to look as if you are pulling these lines out of your head on the fly...which is not too far from the truth. Just file the line away in your head and retrieve it in a month when the situation arises again and everyone has forgotten that they have heard it already.

The internet can be a fantastic tool for the mining of material. Look up jokes in any internet search engine, and you will find more web pages than you will ever be able to read. This can be a great source of one-liners or jokes that you can dissect for punch lines (see Chapter 7).

Another source of good material is sometimes not so obvious-other witty people. You have different social circles that you inhabit-ones with work people, friends, family, a local hangout, etc. There will undoubtedly be people there who are already witty, at least somewhat. And even people who are not normally funny can come out with a good line now and then. Remember these lines...but never use them in the same social circle. You wouldn't like it if you came up with a good line, and before you had used it on a few people, someone else had told it to everyone, would you? Don't do that to someone else. Instead, you can take lines that someone has said in your personal life and use them at work (or the other way around).

Another source actually breaks some of the rules stated above...that source is movie quotes. When using a movie quote, you are using material that many people know, but that's okay, because when you use a movie quote it is in the hope that people *will* recognize the source. The source of humor here lies in the fact that the quote comes at a timely point in the conversation, so that even though the people you are talking to know that the line is not yours, the wittiness comes from the fact that you can recall and deliver the line at the exact point it is needed.

One caveat for movie quotes--they are far more effective when you can do at least a marginal impression of the actor that originally delivered the line. The effect can be humorous even when the line was not originally a funny line. Imagine that you are hosting a dinner for some friends when one of them asks "what's for dinner?". You reply "liver...with some fava beans and a nice chianti." the word liver is said in a normal tone, but the last part is delivered in your best Anthony Hopkins/Hannibal Lecter voice from Silence of the Lambs. An example of a person who does this often is Jim Carrey. A timely movie quote injected into normal conversation can be very witty.

Yet another source of material is probably dropped off at your house every day-the comics in your local papers. Comics are great because they are short and often have some very funny lines that you can inject into everyday situations. Even humor columnists in the paper can be a good source of lines. However, as with any source that a great many people are likely to have access to, timing is an issue. Read a funny line over breakfast and deliver it to your coworkers over lunch, and chances are at least some of them will have also read it that morning. Again, the illusion must be that you are making lines up on your own in order for you to appear witty. This situation can easily be avoided by just storing that line away either in your memory, or write it down for later use. If you give it at least two weeks before you use it, most people will not remember that they knew the line already.

There are other sources all around you if you keep on the lookout for them. I have gotten lines out of little funny quotes in coffee house newspapers, and even bumper stickers. Also, realize that there is another source--yourself. You may not be a comedy writer, but everyone can come up with a few lines here and there that are funny.

The final source of material will be dealt with in the next chapter.

Lab Work

For now, here is an exercise to do…now, you didn't think you were going to get away without doing some homework, did you? Come on, this is your personality we are trying to change here!

Here are some common subjects that come up in everyday conversation. In the next three weeks come up with at least three funny lines for every subject by using the sources of material that we have discussed. These should be funny enough that *you* laughed when you first heard them.

Subject:
1. Doctor/health
2. Work life/boss
3. Recreation/sports
4. Dating/relationships
5. Sex
6. Religion (careful with this one)
7. Politics

Here's an example of material gained from a popular late night talk show. It was a prop joke done during the host's monologue.
"Have you seen those new camera cell phones? The pictures they take are not very good…well, here take a look at these."
At this point the host pulled about five pictures out of his jacket and flipped through them. Every one was a picture of his ear.

In the coming chapters, we will use this example to illustrate the process.

Chapter 7
Jokes are Not Funny

Quotation is a serviceable substitute for wit. -Oscar Wilde

If you are like most people, jokes have been your sole source of material to try and appear as if you are a funny person. Hopefully, by the time you finish this book you will not be like most people anymore. Have you ever known anyone that told a lot of jokes? Did you think that they were witty or did you think that they were boring?

Sit around at a party and tell a few jokes. What happens? After two jokes, most people lose interest. And those two jokes will not get very many laughs. Why is this? As explained earlier, this is because of our old nemesis *expectation*. If a person tells you that they are going to make you laugh, it suddenly becomes a lot more difficult to do so because you now have the expectation that something funny is going to be said.

When a person says "a guy walks into a bar", this triggers a pattern recognition process in your brain. You have heard thousands of jokes in your life, so you can immediately recognize that a joke is being told by the way the language is used. This sets up the expectation in your mind that a punchline is coming, after which you know you will be expected to laugh. Often you *will* laugh--more out of politeness than humor. When you know the punchline is coming it lessens the impact so much that when the line finally comes, it usually doesn't live up to your expectation, therefore the laughs produced are minimal. And what if you have already heard the joke?

They are called punchlines for a reason---it is supposed to be a sudden, sharp sucker punch right to the funny bone. It wouldn't be very effective if George Foreman said to his opponent "Hey, I'm going to deliver a right hook to your ear in about three seconds, okay?" It would be a lot more effective to whip a Foreman Grill out of his trunks and sail it into the other guy's temple. Telling jokes is just a bad idea all around. The answer to this problem is simple. DO NOT TELL JOKES! Again with the shouting, I know. But this is the cardinal rule, and if you learn nothing else from this book, please remember at least this lesson. Never, ever tell a single joke. But, you say, I just read a great joke, I think people would laugh at it, should I just ignore it? The answer is no. Don't ignore the joke if it's funny…use it, but in a very different way--by dissecting the joke. Don't worry, there are no messy internal organs to deal with, and you don't have to kill any frogs (although my school was so rough we dissected custodians instead). Dissecting a joke is a simple procedure, and many witty comments can be derived from this method.

Pretty much ninety percent of any joke is the setup. You waste so much time setting up the situation, that saying the punchline at the end seems almost anticlimactic. How do we avoid this? By taking the punchline out of the joke. After all, that's the funny part, right? The punchline is the only part that you should ever say. When you dissect a joke, you are storing the funny parts in your mind for later use, when you actually find yourself in the situation described.

There are two ways to dissect a joke. One way is to turn the language around so that it relates to you. For example, "a guy walks into a bar" becomes "the last time I was in a bar". When a joke is dissected this way, the conversation itself sets up the joke, and you can inject the punchline into the conversation before they know it is a joke they are hearing. This eliminates the expectation of laughter and catches them off guard...and unexpected comedy is the most powerful producer of laughs. Even if they have heard the joke that the punchline belongs to, they will laugh because you caught them off guard.

Another way to dissect a joke is to wait until you are actually in the situation described by the joke, then inject the punchline into the situation. This is one of the best ways to appear witty, because if you have a punchline for many different situations, it appears as if you are reacting to the world around you on the fly, instead of performing a scripted routine. For example, "a guy goes into a Chinese food restaurant and orders a big meal. He eats all of the food and sits back from the table with a contented sigh. Then he cracks open his fortune cookie and pulls out the fortune which says (*the punchline)*"

This joke is not all that funny on its own, depending on the punchline of course, but it could generate a chuckle or two. However, if you happen to actually be in a Chinese food restaurant with some friends, when the fortune cookie comes to the table everyone inevitably asks what the other fortunes are. If you wait until this moment, and as you pull out yours you say "I hope this fortune is better than the last one I got", their response will of course be "what was the last one". At this point the punchline comes out--"the last one I got said 'I peed in your rice'". This is totally unexpected, and will produce laughter as it sinks in that this was a joke...not only a joke, but one that fit perfectly into the situation you are in, again making it seem like you have a witty line for every situation.

Here's another example of dissecting a joke.

Joke: The pilot and copilot are about to land at LAX, and they are nervous. The sweat is pouring down off their heads as they put the landing gear down. Suddenly the wheels touch the ground and the pilot throws the engines into reverse, he stands on the brakes, he throws up the flaps and they're praying "stop, please stop". The plane just stops in time. The pilot looks at the copilot and says, "that was the shortest runway I've ever seen". The copilot says "yeah, but look how WIDE it is."

All in all, a fairly lame joke. Not too bad, but if you told this joke to someone they probably wouldn't laugh very much. Now let's dissect it. The only important part of the joke is that the runway is short, but very wide. The rest of the joke is setup only. When you dissect a joke, you are taking only the funny parts, (most of the time just the punchline) and injecting it into either a real-life situation or a conversation about a real-life situation. Easy, right? Let me explain. An example of a real-life situation would be that a friend (or coworker, or even taxi driver) is picking you up at the airport. You have just gotten off of a plane, and the natural first question asked of you is "how was your flight?" Even without this opening, you can still say "the landing was really scary, that airport has the shortest runway I've ever seen. But it was really, really *wide*.

In the case of a conversation, it would be someone talking about a trip they went on when you say "the last time my plane almost didn't land...the runway was very short, but really *wide*. Now you have added the punchline into a conversation, at the appropriate time.

Lab Work

Guess what time it is? That's right, homework time again. Search the internet or joke books for some jokes that would be good to dissect. Once you have a workable witty line, add that to your list under the appropriate topic heading. Do at least five.

Now let's go back to our example from the talk show. In that case the joke relied on having the pictures as a prop. Obviously, it would be ridiculous to carry around pictures on the off chance that someone might bring up the subject of camera cell phones, so instead we can dissect it. Instead of the props, we can take just the *idea* that the only pictures you took were of your ear. We will refine this basic idea in an upcoming chapter.

Chapter 8
Refining the Material

I fear nothing so much as a man who is witty all day long. -Madame de Sevigne

Not every line that you hear will be comedy gold. Some might be comedy aluminum, or even some kind of nickel-lead alloy. This is where refining the material comes in.

Refining the material and delivery have a lot in common. The goal in each is to come up with the very best way to say a particular line that will produce the maximum amount of amusement. There are a few different ways to go about this.

The first thing to do is to say the line aloud a few times. Experiment by putting the emphasis on different syllables, rearranging the words, or substituting different words. Or just take the idea and say it completely different in your own words. A good tool to use for this is the old standby, the thesaurus. There's no need to overdo it, but sometimes by changing just one word it makes the impact of the line greater because your listeners were not expecting that particular word in the context of the conversation you were having. For example, if you go back to the fortune cookie example, I was going to say as the punchline "I spit in your rice." In playing around with it I realized that "I peed in your rice" is just a whole lot more amusing.

In the end you may realize that the line was best the way you originally heard it or thought it up. It really doesn't matter if you change it or not, as long as you end up with something in the end that strikes you as the best way to say it.

Lab Work

Your only work this time is to take the list of lines you have and go over each one, altering if necessary to make each one funnier.

Now let's come back to our example. We have the idea that a camera cell phone only takes pictures of your ear. Now we need a way to say that in the best possible way. So let's try out a few ways of saying it.

"I had a camera phone once. But all I ever got were pictures of my ear."

"My camera phone just took pictures of my ear."

"I had one, but I never learned to use it. I got a lot of pictures of my ear, though."

You get the idea. Try it any way you can think of, you never know when you will hit upon one that sounds better than the rest. Play around with it, pick one of these or make your own line up. Once you have the line down the way you want it, practice saying it a few times so that you know the delivery. Now you can deliver the line the next time the subject comes up.

Chapter 9
Creating Opportunity

He is winding the watch of his wit; by and by it will strike. -William Shakespeare

Now that you have all of this good material, you need a place to use it, right? This is where the opportunity part of the formula comes in.

When you first start out, you will have to wait for opportunities to present themselves. This happens more often than you might think, and if you just rely on it happening by itself you can still appear witty. However, the more comments you can make (to a point, of course) the more witty you will appear. There are a lot of people who can come out with a line here and there. Our goal here is not to be like a lot of people, but to stand out from the crowd. The best way to do this is by making your own opportunities.

One of the first things to start doing when you begin the process of becoming witty is to start *listening*. It sounds simple, but this is one of the hardest things for people to do. Here's a news flash for you--when the average person is in a conversation, they are merely waiting for the other person to stop speaking so that they can make their next point. That's right, they are not really listening because they are focusing their attention on formulating their next point or story. Realize that you probably do this as well, and realize that this is a habit that it would be a good idea to break. Once you are aware of this habit and control it, you can begin to *actively listen*.

When you start actively listening, you do two things. First, the other person becomes aware that you actually might be interested in the fact that their great aunt's cousin's dog once ate out of Harrison Ford's garbage, which makes them feel important. Actively listening is just good human relations. Second, when you are really listening, you can start to see the direction a conversation is headed…and start to line up material for use when it gets there. I know, I know, I just went against everything I just told you. How can you line up material and listen at the same time? This takes some practice, but it can be done. Listening and trying to come up with a line you can use all at once is tricky, so don't try to do both just yet. For now, practice really listening to conversations that are taking place around you every day. Try to guess what subjects will come up, but don't try to inject some witty material at this point…learn to walk before you run. Once you have a good deal of material learned, and you know how to listen for the opportunities, then you can start to think about the lines you would say while you are listening to a conversation.

A word about a little something I call 'cultural literacy'. Cultural literacy is what I call the knowledge of current events, TV shows, movies, big news stories, anything that makes its way into common knowledge.

It is not hard to stay culturally literate, but it does take some time to keep it up. Having cultural literacy is a huge advantage when you are trying to be witty. It means that you have a greater base of material that is topical and fresh, and you can make references to many different things that a large variety of people will recognize. Just imagine saying a movie quote perfectly, that fits the situation, and you think is hysterically funny. If it's from a movie that was only shown once in a bamboo theater in Bora Bora for an audience of five people that didn't understand English, chances are pretty good that nobody's going to get the reference.

So how do we stay culturally literate? Become voracious in your consumption of media. Watch a lot of TV, especially the popular shows, see a lot of movies, even if you wait for them to come to DVD. Most people rent to see movies anyway, so any reference won't be well received until some time after the video release. Get on the internet! Internet fads like the 'Star Wars Kid' or 'All Your Base Are Belong To Us' become part of the popular culture, in some cases just as much as shows like Seinfeld do, depending on the group you happen to be talking to. Anything that becomes part of popular culture is something that you can reference for laughs. Even funny or in some cases annoying commercials can be referenced. Just think how you could have saved face if you had ever slipped on the ice in front of your friends and instead of getting embarrassed you came out with a quote from that old commercial "I've fallen and I can't get up". They would have laughed with you, not at you. Or when your boyfriend dropped his pants you could have said "Where's the beef!". Screaming laughter all around. Well, not for him. Both of these are very dated references now of course, but you get the idea. Cultural literacy just means keeping your eyes and ears open for anything that a lot of people are likely to have seen.

Another good thing to do to create opportunities is something you probably do every morning...read the newspaper. This is one of the best ways to appear witty, because you can sit in the comfort of your own home with your list of lines and relate them to the news of the day. Then later when you go to work or meet with your friends, you can pretty much guarantee that the conversation will eventually turn to the news stories that you have lines for, and if it doesn't, you can easily bring up the subject as casual discussion of current events. Nobody will ever suspect that you had all the time in the world to come up with something funny to say for the headlines. To them, it will look as if you just made them up on the spot, even if you brought the subject up yourself!

Lab Work

Now, time for your homework. Alright, stop whining, it's easy. This is not brain science, or rocket surgery, it's the science of wit. At this point, you have the list of five topics with the three lines each from the first lab work, and the jokes you dissected from the second assignment, because you *did* do your homework, didn't you? Don't make me come down there.

This assignment is not nearly as hard as the other ones. All you have to do is actively listen to the conversations around you during the next few days or so. Remember the five topics you have and just make a mental note each time one of those topics comes up in the conversation. That's it. Simply recognize each topic as it comes up. Once you have done this a few times, start to play a little mental game with yourself to try to guess which topic will come up next. After a few times, you will be surprised how many times you guess correctly. Once you have this down, start trying to recall the lines you have for these topics. Don't say them yet—just make a mental note of them. This will make good practice for the next chapter.

Once you are comfortable with doing this, you can try for the mastery level--try to gently steer the conversation towards a topic you pick. Don't do this in a sudden way, the key word here is *gently*. There has to be a smooth transition between one topic and another or it will look and feel awkward to you and the other people. Be smart, don't bring up sex when other people are talking about the ham sandwich they had for lunch (unless you run with a very strange crowd). Again, don't try to inject any witty comments at this point--remember to learn to walk before you run.

Pick a topic that you want to steer the conversation toward. Now wait for an opening. If you are listening to what's going on in the conversation, you should be able to see an opportunity to relate something in your chosen topic to the current topic being discussed. This is where your cultural literacy really comes in handy.

Once again let's go back to our example. If you were practicing cultural literacy, you would have seen that late night talk show with the joke about the camera cell phones. Your task is to try to steer the conversation to a subject that is somehow related to the subject of cell phones, or even camera cell phones. Do not be obvious about it, try to make it subtle. For example, if they are talking about technology in general you can bring up an ad you saw for a camera that was the size of a credit card. Someone at this point will probably bring up the cell phone cameras, or you can then bring them up yourself. Don't say anything about the joke, just bring up the topic to practice doing it.

All conversation is like a constantly moving train. It is easy to see that by having a high degree of cultural literacy, it becomes a lot easier to make the different connections between topics. Sometimes you have to go through one topic to make it to another. It's just a matter of laying down the right tracks and switches to make the train stop at your station. Try not to derail it. Can I stop with the train analogy now, or would you like me to engineer another one?

Once you are proficient with your listening and conversation skills, you will find that you have a new confidence when you are engaged in conversation. Even if you stop at this point and don't take it further, you will have already gained a good set of social skills.

Chapter 10
Total Recall

It may be said that his wit shines by the help of his memory. -Alain René Le Sage

There are many books out there on how to improve memory. It is not my intention to paraphrase these books here (mostly because I don't remember their titles), but as memory plays such a big part in being witty, it must be mentioned. Some of these books on improving memory include little tricks to "associate" one thing to another.

To illustrate this, imagine that you meet someone named Tom and you need to remember his name. You could write it down, but that's not always a practical solution because most of the time when you meet someone new you are standing up. You could repeat his name over and over as you talk to him, but after a while he might start to think that you're a few sandwiches short of a picnic. Instead, one of the things you can try is to find some characteristic about his physical appearance to try to associate to his name. For example, if you look at his face and it just happens to remind you of the way a turtle's face looks, you could try to associate in your mind the two terms by making a mental note along the lines of "Tom the turtle". This way, the next time you see the person, you would look at his face and think to yourself "he looks like a turtle-it must be Tom the turtle". Thus, you remember that his name is Tom by using this method, which works just fine until the one day when you see him and say "Hi, Turtle Face". Seriously though, this type of method can work well as a system for remembering things.

For our purposes, this system is perfect because we already have two things to associate-a topic and a witty line. Now, this is where being witty starts to look a little like work. I know, I know, I used the W word. But you don't have to dig a ditch, you just have to learn a few lines. Being witty takes on some of the same characteristics as being an actor at this point, the only difference being the amount of lines you have to memorize. Just imagine how many lines an actor has to learn to do one Broadway play or one movie. You have a lot less to learn than that, so don't worry, it is easily done.

Repetition out loud is one of the best ways to remember lines, and it also helps you hone the material. By testing out different ways to say the lines, you can also come up with the ideal presentation for each one. This is one of the things comedians do, and being witty could be described as a cross between an actor and a comedian. The only difference is that you don't have to do it up on a stage. That's a big plus for those people with stage fright like me.

Not only do you need to learn the lines themselves, but you also have to associate each line with its topic. This step is really done at the same time as learning your lines, because what the line says directly relates to the topic. Sometimes, there is more than one topic to associate to. For example, in the line "I gave up bowling for sex, the balls are lighter and you don't have to change your shoes" you can associate both bowling and sex so that when either subject comes up you can deliver the line. Once the lines are in your head, you will see how easy it is to be reminded of them when a topic comes up in conversation.

Lab Work

Homework time! You know you want it. Calculate the entrance vector of the shuttle from a moon trajectory of—no, no, this is not that hard, people! Take your list of funny lines (you have one, right?) and associate each line with its topic. You can do this by reading the list over and over, you can do it by trying to write them out from memory, you can do it by saying them into a tape recorder or even do it with flash cards. Some people say them while looking into a mirror. Personally, I have a weak stomach, so I don't really want to look at myself, but whatever floats your boat. Just do whatever works best for you, but there are a few things to remember.

First, go over each line and work out the best way to say it. You've already gone over these lines when refining the material, but sometimes when you say them it doesn't quite work out. So change a word if you think it's more funny, relate it to something closer to you by inserting the name of someone or a group, whatever you have to do to make it funnier. Or it might be funny enough on its own. In many cases, if the material came from a stand-up comedian, it has already been honed in this way, so it's best to leave it alone. Once you have the line formulated in the correct way, practice saying it so that it becomes automatic. If you do this with enough lines, you will have a good catalog of material that you can use more than once in your different circles of friends, coworkers and relatives.

Also, try to associate each line not only with its topic, but specific things about the topic...for example, for politics if the line only works with one politician, try to associate it to them.

Time to go back to our example. Just associate the topic of cell phone cameras to pictures of your ear. That's it! Just associate the two subjects in your mind so that one reminds you of the other. Don't worry about the actual line you will say, we will get to that next chapter.

Chapter 11
Delivery

Wit ought to be a glorious treat like caviar; never spread it about like marmalade. -Noel Coward

Delivery is very important. There are a number of different ways that you can deliver a witty line, ranging from a deadpan delivery, to sarcastic and even non sequitur. Fed Ex is also an option, but that's only if it has to be there overnight.

A deadpan delivery works very well. If you are acting like you are about to tell a joke, laughing or chuckling, then expectation is heightened. Remember, the best laughs come from no expectation. A deadpan delivery results when you act like what you are saying has no humor whatsoever, which results in confusion and therefore bigger laughs.

A sarcastic delivery is often very effective, but again, use it sparingly. Often, sarcasm is best used when doing lines that are self-deprecating. Right, like *I'm* smart enough to know what *that* means.

Non sequitur is a latin phrase meaning "it does not follow". This kind of delivery needs no setup whatsoever. A non sequitur line is something you just blurt out, for no reason at all, and it has nothing to do with the current conversation or the conversation that just happened. Non sequiturs can be good for filling a gap in the conversation, or when there is no conversation at all. An example of a good non sequitur can be suddenly starting to sing a funny song, or coming out with a movie quote at the right time. I'll give you an example. The other day I was with a group of people at a new building that just opened up. The escalators were not functioning yet, so we were faced with having to walk up a fair number of stairs. As we were going up, I was reminded of the famous scene in the movie Rocky where Sylvester Stallone is running up the stairs. There was no conversation as we were going up, so when we were about halfway I pumped my fists in the air and did an impression of Stallone saying "Adrian! Adrian!". Everyone laughed because it was totally out of the blue, yet very topical to the situation we were in. As I said in the last chapter, if your material is from a standup comedian, often the best thing to do is to deliver the line in the same way they do in their act. Remember, comedians are very good at what they do, and their lines are always honed to receive the largest amount of laughs by exposure to a wide variety of different audiences, so it's usually best to do it the same as they do. If the lines are from different sources, then work out the way to say it that seems funniest to you before you say it. This step should have already been done in the refining the material part of the formula in Chapter 8, but to recap, say it aloud to yourself in a few different ways. Try putting the emphasis on different syllables, try different words to say the same thing, anything to make the line sound more amusing.

One more thing about delivery. One of the most important things is to KNOW YOUR AUDIENCE. This cannot be stressed enough. Jokes about politics, religion or sex can be very funny, but if you say them in the wrong company not only will you not be popular, but you might just wind up eating through a straw for the next few months!

Chapter 12
Putting it All Together

Wit makes it own welcome and levels all distinctions. -Ralph Waldo Emerson

Let's recap what you've learned so far. By now, you should be able to gather material from various sources. You should also be able to actively listen to a conversation and determine what direction it is headed. You may even be able to steer the conversation to a topic that you pick. These represent the first two parts of our formula – **Material** and **Opportunity**.

Now it's time to step up to the plate. By now you should also have a list of lines that has been associated to topics in your mind. You should know these lines by memorizing them. This the **Recall** part of the formula. Now it's time to test out your **Delivery**.

If you have gone over all of your lines, you should have a way to deliver each one that sounds funny to you. Now you can start to say witty comments as the subjects come up in conversation. You've done a lot of work to get to this point, but as far as the outside world is concerned, your transformation to a witty person is only just beginning. This is where a lot of people go wrong. The goal here is to *slowly* change into that witty person, not completely change your outward personality in one day. Show some restraint! Use only a few lines here and there at first until your confidence builds.

As you use your skills more and more, you will find a strange thing happening--it gets easier and easier to remember and deliver your lines. It may seem like a lot of work at first, but after a while it will come naturally, and you will feel yourself actually turning into the witty person that you always wanted to be.

Of course, you can't stop at the lines you came up with when doing your lab work. You must constantly come up with new material. At first this will be a little bit of work, but now that you know what to look for in material, you will notice that you start to pick it up everywhere you go. You will find as you do this that the material comes to you easier all the time, and the whole process starts to become automatic. After a few weeks, your transformation will be complete.

Congratulations! You are now well on your way to becoming a witty person. I'm sorry I don't have a cap and gown for you, but you never really graduate from this course. It is an ongoing learning process, but every day it gets easier until it becomes second nature to you. The important thing is that you have attempted to change. This fact alone is often enough to help facilitate the transformation. In the next chapter you will learn the final lesson that you need to know before you are set loose on an unsuspecting world.

Chapter 13
Knowing When to Quit

To be witty is not enough. One must possess sufficient wit to avoid having too much of it. -Andre Maurois

As the quote says, being witty is not enough. You must also possess the wisdom to use your powers for good, not evil. Remember, there can be too much of a good thing. If you don't believe me, try eating an entire case of Hershey's Kisses sometime.

Obviously, there are certain social situations where trying to be witty can hurt you instead of helping you. Try to exercise your common sense and judgment. Don't joke with the officer who's giving you a ticket. Don't try to make witty comments about bombs at the airport. Don't try to work the room at a funeral, even if the first three letters of funeral are fun. All common sense things you wouldn't do, of course. But even though our goal is to have lightning fast lines for any situation, you should never forget to think before speaking.

For starters, try to remember if the group you are with has already heard the line from you...this is not always easy to remember, but you will find that you can get good at making educated guesses about it. If you are talking to strangers, try not to make off-color remarks until you know what their sense of humor is like.

There is also a point when even well-received witty remarks get old. As I said earlier, Mike was very good at what he did, but I found that being at that level was a little too much for me. Just as I did, you have to find the level that feels most comfortable to you. Learn to walk the fine line between being witty and "always trying to be the center of attention". You don't have to have a funny comment to everything. Remember, people love to laugh, but they also love to be heard...always make time to listen to the conversation.

Well, that's it. In a few weeks all of these steps will have become an automatic process, and you will find yourself getting new friends and meeting people easier. Be proud of yourself! Changing your innate personality is not an easy task, but I hope that I have made the transition as easy as I could have. Now get out there and make 'em laugh!

Appendix 1

Here are some lines that I have used in the past that you can use to get you started.

Doctor

Last time I went there the tongue depressor tasted like a popsicle.
My Prozac comes in colors and it has a little "M" on each pill.
Instead of Viagra he gave me a popsicle stick and some duct tape.

Religion

I'm a First Mechanist—I go to Our Lady of Perpetual Motion church
I'm a dyslexic agnostic – that means I don't believe in dog
If money is the root of all evil, why do churches beg for it?
My karma ran over my dogma

Work Life

As soon as you put on a tie, it cuts the oxygen to the brain...that's why management is so stupid
I've been disgruntled employee of the month for 60 straight months
I like to go to work naked...it diverts attention from the fact that I also go in drunk

I hurt my back taking a management course… it's not easy trying to put your head up your ass

School

I'm training to be an amateur gynecologist (or, in the case of someone asking what you do for a living… I'm an amateur gynecologist)

My school was rough, we didn't have recess, we had cease fire

I'm in the half of the class that makes the top half possible

Self-deprecating

I have a washboard stomach—I just have a little laundry on it right now, that's all

I'm hung like Einstein and smart as a horse

Insult

(Pointing to target person, but talking to someone else) You see what happens when cousins marry?

I remember when I had my first beer, too

Your mother must be proud of you, you've got all those extra chromosomes

If his IQ was 3 points higher he'd be a geranium

He's as sharp as a marble

Printed in Great Britain
by Amazon

34786532R00020